Th
Entrepreneur's Almanack

by

Robin Bennett

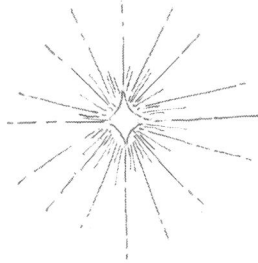

Illustrations *by* Jude Bennett

The Entrepreneur's Almanack
(Monster Books Ltd).

Originally published in Great Britain
by Monster Books, The Old Smithy,
Henley-on-Thames, Oxon. RG9 2AR.
Published in November 2025.

The right of Robin Bennett to be identified
as author of this work has been asserted by
him in accordance with the Copyright,
Designs and Patents Act 1988.

Text copyright Robin Bennett.
Illustration copyright Jude Bennett.

A catalogue record of this book is available
from the British Library.
Design and typeset
medievalbookshop.co.uk.

Printed by Amazon

To all free marketeers.

"Unlike cynicism, hopefulness is hard-earned,
it makes demands on us.
Hopefulness is adversarial,
it is the warrior emotion."
Nick Cave

Antelogium

This third in a series of short yearbooks is about entrepreneurship and a key aspect of the same, which is steadfastly
overlooked in my experience. And it boils down to this: success
in business has more to do with intangibles than we care to
admit.

By that I mean things you can't quite pin down, rather feel—
for example, the guesswork and gut that make up a large part of
our biggest decisions. The hard-nosed business collective
stoutly refuses to have any truck with such things, but I disagree.

And it doesn't stop there: the *soul* in a business venture, the
divine providence, even dumb luck are all players and should be
welcomed round the table, not ignored at the fringes. Investing
in this idea has undeniably paid off for me in several businesses:
from translation to tuition, cigars to sandwiches, publishing,
dog kennels, gold trading and gardening. But for a belief in
benign fate coming to the rescue, I'm quite sure I'd have thrown
in the towel more than once and gone to work nine to five
somewhere grim.

So, I hope the Entrepreneur's Almanack can help increase
your chances of success in whatever business you decide is for
you—and be entertaining at the same time. I think levity and a
sense that everything is far from terrible—even when anyone
with a modicum of sense would say it is—engenders good
fortune. I don't know how or why that is, but I find it to be so.

The Entrepreneur's Almanack is a cosmic crutch, plus glee.

Sometime during the last tranche of 1987, I was sauntering along
one of the slightly insalubrious backstreets that take you from
the relative bustle of Covent Garden to the unequivocal mayhem that is Trafalgar Square.

I had an interview with a man at the MOD in officers' offices above Admiralty Arch.

Partly the fact I was dressed like a toff and a great deal because I also looked young and therefore gullible, a square set man—like a modern version of Bill Sykes—picked me out of the crowd.

'Old Moore's Almanack?' he asked, except the way he said it came out *Olmursarmagnac* ... like he was offering me a drink. Then his hand, like a small bear's paw, shoved a pamphlet under my nose. At first glance it looked like the cover of a playbill: a minor explosion of differing fonts and caps. The man and the book seemed to go together: of another age, a bit peculiar, a bit intriguing.

'Um what?' I said.

'Old Moore's Almanack,' he repeated, as if that was quite enough explanation to be getting on with.

I stared at him until he realised he might have to do better than that.

'It's got predictions, all you need to know n'that. I saw you marching down the street like a guard's officer and thought there's a lad with his future ahead of him.'

So, I bought a copy, which just goes to prove his own prediction was right: I am gullible.

Everybody's future is ahead of them.

January

INSIGNIS

The month of January is named in honour of one of the few uniquely Roman gods, Janus. Sometimes called two-faced, as in not very trustworthy, I prefer the view that he is symbolic of beginnings and endings, as well as the god of gates and doorways. Paths to the past and to the future.

January is one of the top months for businesspeople to be born according to statistics sourced, somewhat randomly, online. It's also the least likely birth month you'll wind up an estate agent, according to the same set of data. Make of that what you will.

It is the month of Capricorn (progeny of a daddy goat that fell in love with a mummy fish). Amongst their many good and bad traits that work well in business (hard-working, practical, honest, stubborn, with a tendency towards being suspicious), they are said to age backwards—becoming more upbeat and optimistic as they get older.

Try and be more like a sea goat.

Datus

Marketing

4th National Trivia Day
6th Epiphany, the day of revelation
13th National Make your Dream come
True Day
18th International Winnie the Pooh
Day (also Get to know your Customers
Day)
26th National Fun at Work Day

Boring Stuff (UK)

31st Deadline for filing and paying
self-assessment tax returns.
31st Capital Gains Tax Balancing
payment
31st First payment on account for
Income Tax

Auspicious time for

Planning
Planting crops (Ch)
Tearing Down a building (Ch)
Surgery (Ch)

Beware!

Depression (so be careful what you
give up)
Stove installation (Ch)
Building a door (Ch)

Birthday of Famous Entrepreneur

Jeff Bezos

Birthday of Inspiring person you've never heard of

Peter Mark Roget
Former doctor, created or possibly
originated, even conceived the first
English Thesaurus

Special mention
Pete Harman

Founding partner of KFC and the chap
who coined 'Kentucky Fried Chicken'.
Best of all, he invented the bucket.
Genius.

'Ch' = Chinese predictions, which I find to be eerily specific and perhaps all the
more accurate for that.

Decreta
CANNOT FAIL FACTOR NUMBER ONE

Following my encounter in the West End and fast forwarding to 1992, which was when I started my first business, I could have done with a few signposts. Celestial or otherwise. I really hadn't got a clue. In fact, that's an understatement—in terms of business acumen, I was a danger to myself and others.

Fifteen start-ups and over thirty years later, I know a bit more about the world of entrepreneurship. Very far from everything—I still don't grasp anything but the most rudimentary accounting—but enough to know one important thing that routinely gets overlooked in the maelstrom of cashflow forecasts, focus groups and feasibility studies. And it's this: if you lack for a set of determinations that gives your business a forthright purpose, a pathway and a psyche, you're missing the point. And not just in entrepreneurship, in any human endeavour I'd venture. I'm going to dub them *Decreta*.

And by that I don't mean a mere plan—*Decreta* are more resolutions plus confidence—a call to arms you do first, before you get your coloured Planning Pens out. They are essential because otherwise all you've got is a grand-sounding to-do list—a list which will get shoved to one side the minute there is a minor drama at home or it suddenly seems preferable to walk the dog.

In fact, plot is also a useful word here because I've noticed that the best businesses—the ones that work against the odds, overriding the inevitable calamities along the way—strongly rely on a structure that is very similar to a decent narrative.

Bear with me on this.

The classic (and classical) Five Act structure of a story has been used in almost all the great plays, books, films—anything that relays what it is to be human. It requires:

1. a call to action: a goal to overcome,
2. vicissitudes of this going well,

3. then not so well ...
4. ... a crisis and
5. a crisis overcome = a happy ending.

This is life, or life as we want it, so it resonates. There's a reason why both work: they make sense to us and they speak to the heart ... and that attracts others: be they readers, viewers, customers or **clients**.

This is also why your company needs clear character (like in a book—a marketing identity, if you will), a good backstory that enables the 'call to action' (the essential **why this business?** question).

Solid *Decreta* are one of the Cannot Fail Factors every business needs.

For me, back then with my bottle green moped and my mini Matterhorn student debt, I certainly needed money but I was keen to work with words, they'd always been my friend— whether that was communication: of knowledge and ideas or stories, I didn't feel picky. And that is how London Tutors (home tuition), Aktuel Translations (translation) and Monster Books (publishing) were started almost concurrently, between January and March of that horribly-cold winter.

This is daft, most people who could be bothered to have an opinion about me said why start three companies before the first gets off the ground? Do it in stages. That's the sensible, grown-up option. But it didn't fit with my *Decreta*, because I already had a group of companies in my mind—The Bennett Group—and it had a strapline, *Life's a Banquet*. I was going to be eclectic; I was out to prove a point that you could be somewhat unfocussed, seemingly light-weight, hyperactive and still make a go of it. Above all, I was going to have some fun.

Anyway, on 8th January 1992, I sat down in the glacial upper deck study of the houseboat in Chelsea where I was living and remember jotting down something along these lines ...

1. What is the point of my business within the context of the rest of my life? Does it plot?
2. Back story? People love a back story.

3. Now drill down to a proper set of strategies and a cashflow forecast.
4. Stick to the these.
5. Within reason.
6. Regularly assess things on the following criteria
   a) Is the plan working?
   b) Am I happy?
   c) Are people around me happy?
   d) Can I easily remember why I am doing this (seven second rule)?
7. Make time for whatever it is I like to do as if I have all the time in the world.
8. Within reason.
9. Finish the year better off—spiritually, but mainly in cash terms.
10. Don't cheat people.
11. Always have a reason for doing anything from here on in. Prevarication is the great enemy of entrepreneurship.
12. Never forget this.

Looking back after thirty-five years, this was about the only thing I got right in those early days.

February
INSIGNIS

Named after festival of Purification, Februa and it is the third and last month of meteorological winter in the Northern Hemisphere. Unlucky as it has twenty-eight days according to Romans (though they never said why), but it's generally considered a good month to start something new—even terribly pure—which works for the purpose of this narrative if you're prepared to write off month one (January) as a planning month. It's not a bad shout as nothing much seems to be going on in February after the Christmas rush. Once you've yanked down the Christmas decorations, burned the tree and taken the foot spa you were given to the neighbour's wheelie bin, then you might as well get on with something new—like founding a business empire!

Challenge: Aim for the creativity of a Pisces and self-reliance of an Aquarius.

Datus

*"January is always a good month for behavioral (sic) economics:
Few things illustrate self-control as vividly as New Year's
resolutions. February is even better, though, because it lets us study
why so many of those resolutions are broken."*

Sendhil Mullainathan

Marketing

International Canned Food Month
National Return Shopping Trolleys to
Shops Month
Most likely month to host Chinese
New Year
2nd Groundhog Day (USA, possibly
Canada)
6th National Work Naked Day
14th Valentine's Day (milk it—
everyone else does)
17th Random Act of Kindness Day
22nd National Margarita Day (the
cocktail, not the pizza—that's in June)

Boring Stuff (UK)

If your company's financial year ends
on 30th April Year X, the deadline for
paying your corporation tax is 01
February the following year, Y.
If it doesn't, kick back and relax after
all the returns mayhem in January.
Have a Margarita/Margherita.

Auspicious time for

Shopping trolleys
Purity, perhaps
Love, obviously
Take a Bath (Ch)
Haircut (Ch)

Beware!

Naked people popping up at work on
or around 6th
Getting married (Ch)
Building a ship (Ch)

Birthday of Famous Entrepreneur

Steve Jobs (and Dr. Dre [not really a
doctor])

Birthday of Inspiring person you've probably never heard of

Cleisthenes
True father of democracy

Special mention

Peter Freuchen
6ft 7in Explorer, writer, badass and
everything in between. Once used his
own faeces to fashion a trenching tool
to escape an avalanche.

Primitia
GETTING DOWN TO THE NITTY GRITTY

My life in London was framed by parks in those early days. Over the previous summer and autumn, I'd found a job as a 'gardener' looking after Shepherd's Bush Green. I'd got fit cycling six miles to work each day to pick up litter, strim tussocks of grass mined with dog poo and water sad planters on the roundabout that marked the boundary between the gentility of Notting Hill Gate and the badlands of Shepherd's Bush. In my lunch hours, I sat under the trees in the memorial garden plotting what I was going to do with the rest of my life now I'd burned my bridges on becoming a soldier. Bit by bit, I scraped together a couple of grand that would hopefully be enough to start this clutch of small businesses.

Planning and preparation over, by February it was time to start to try and make money. I was still very much aware—but, luckily, not overly—that I was making it up as I went along.

Thus, the grimmest month saw me trying to figure out how you actually make money from a small business (or three), with virtually no cash, in the dregs of a recession.

Battersea Park started and finished my day. I was renting a room perched on the top deck of a houseboat in Chelsea and— the first foothold of my empire—I also rented a flaking desk in the corner of a community centre office near Clapham Junction. The Doddington and Rollo Community Centre was stationed where it was needed, amidst the expanses of council high rises and local initiatives.

On dry days, the park was alive with people and pets. When it was damp and drear, I had the place to myself, which suited me fine.

Back on my houseboat, there was a cormorant who'd balance himself on an oil drum midstream. I'd watch him most days from the deck as I sipped my coffee: either drying his wings in the pale winter sun, black and ragged against the gilt edged ripples of current ... and forbidding; or wrapped up against the drizzle, like an Edwardian in a long coat.

Mostly I admired him: his independence and his toughness was something to emulate.

Initially, carrying things out you told your friends you'd do whilst holding forth in the pub was the order of those days. And staying the course. This felt like the real start of things, I'd broken through the norm of graduate trainee jobs, and I was staring into the breach. But it was also tempting to hedge my bets. In fact, I was to start with, by snatching at easy cash jobs of gardening, home tuition and writing the odd article. These alone were bringing in enough to keep me in red wine and meat, with a roof over my head—albeit a rocky one whose bath filled up with grey-green river water the very next high tide if I forgot to put the plug back in.

But I was also getting into the freewheeling habit of being an entrepreneur and enjoying it. For the first time in my life, I was using my time—pretty much all my time that I wasn't eating, sleeping or socialising—to get on with things with no boss to calibrate my expectations for me. This usually took the form of indirect marketing. And some of it was working, mainly by way of small commissions earned from other tutors with London Tutors, the one of the three that took off quickest. But progress still felt slow.

Walking across the park one day wrapped up in my thoughts, as usual, I had a moment of clarity: I had to commit to this venture—it was time to stop pussy-footing.

So, those side hustles went.

March

INSIGNIS

March symbolises transformation. I'm guessing after Jan and Feb that, for most of us, any month is going to seem pretty lively. March is the month of daffodils and those other ones that aren't quite daffodils and that means it's already got a lot going for it in my book.

Named after Mars, the god of war because, with all this warm weather, farmers could not only start farming again but warriors could get on with pillaging them.

March's Month Stone is the aquamarine, which is a lucky charm for sailors but also has the ability to calm tempers and stir up epiphanies. Now, this is relevant, especially as its birthstone 'buddy' is the bloodstone, which augurs and, presumably, augments bravery.

That the entrepreneur requires valour, goes without saying, but none of that matters if you don't have the odd bout of insight to spur it along.

Datus

Wisdom

"In March winter is holding back and spring is pulling forward. Something holds and something pulls inside of us too."

Jean Hersey

....

Marketing

National Breast Implant Awareness Month (vitally important, given how little attention they get)
6th Day of the Dude (ref The Big Lebowski)
10th International Bagpipe Day
17th St Patrick's Day, of course
19th International Client's Day
25th International Day of Solidarity with Missing Staff Members

Boring Stuff (UK)

31st March Corporation Tax due from previous year if your company tax year spans April-April.

Auspicious time for

Bulbs, boobs and bagpipes (apparently)
Sign a Contract (Ch)
Encoffining (Ch)

Beware!

The Ides of March (especially if you're a Roman senator)
Digging a Well (Ch)

Birthday of Famous Entrepreneur

Lord Sugar, Also Alexander Graham Bell

Birthday of Inspiring Person you've never heard of

Joseph-Nicéphore Niépce
Inventor of photography and the combustion engine (you might also want to look up his brother, Claude)

Special Mention

Dr Joseph Priestley, scientist who discovered oxygen in 1774. His colleagues found him to be a breath of fresh air

Syne Qua Non
CANNOT FAIL FACTOR NUMBER TWO

I had swapped my crap moped for a crap motorbike shortly after I started the business, the better to make meetings on time and not rely on the Tube, which was getting too expensive for my dwindling purse, anyway. It was a monstrous trial bike: heavy, ugly and the rear exhaust would pop off at odd moments, like a party trick, so it went from sounding like a small tractor to very large lorry at inconvenient moments.

Unfortunately, when the bike's MOT came up, what should have been an obvious truth (but one I had successfully ignored) presented itself. Without my secondary incomes—the ones I had given up in order to seem all cool and independent—there wasn't enough money coming in to cover a trip to the supermarket, let alone anything else.

The fact was, three months into my new venture, I was going bust.

And this was only one of a few of my problems. Secondly, I was nursing a broken heart. Two weeks before, my girlfriend of five years had told me it was all over. She still loved me very much, she explained as we walked along the street in Clapham, but things changed. She wasn't wrong about that; things were changing very rapidly indeed. All of them for the worse.

Thirdly, my mother rang to say she was looking out of an upstairs window whilst bailiffs removed cars and furniture. The family business, a fish production plant in Scotland, had pipped mine to the post of ignominy and gone into full liquidation.

Shortly after, I was out on the motorbike. It was early and my mind was probably dwelling on the list of bad things that had been happening to me in a very short space of time. This was why I didn't immediately notice the police car trailing me until the blues and twos were switched on. Once I had been hauled to one side along the Thames Embankment, they explained what the problem was from their perspective. The bike was in such a state of disrepair it could not move another inch. It would have to be left on the side of the road for collection by trained professionals. They took my details. I would be hearing from them via the Crown Prosecution Service, as this was too serious a matter to be dealt with by points and a roadside fine.

To recap, then, my family was facing financial Armageddon, my only means of transport was being impounded and I was looking at a conviction and a fine I wouldn't be able to pay because my business was going bust before it had even started. And the one person I wanted to phone for comfort I couldn't because I was no longer her emotional responsibility.

I leaned against the cold stone of the Embankment and looked out across the choppy, grey water.

And I felt very sorry for myself indeed.

In reality, the last two years had been a series of very bad decisions: from a nice career in a posh regiment I'd turned my back on, interesting job with a music magazine, to door-to-door sales, to working in a shop, then being a council gardener and now about to go bust before I'd had an ounce of tangible success. Each move I'd made looked very much like my foot had missed the ladder and landed on a snake—and I only had myself to blame.

The wind got up and, out of the corner of my eye, I could see the policeman giving me an odd look. I don't think he stopped many people who wandered off, whilst he was filling in the forms, in order to philosophise with themselves.

It wouldn't mend my broken heart, but as I walked back along the Embankment back to the boat, I knew I really had no choice: I had to get something good out of this terrible fuck-up. And that meant I had to find a way to make the business work. Fast.

And that was probably the biggest factor ensuring I did.

April

INSIGNIS

March might be all about Ides, but April also has a lot to be pissed off with Ancient Rome about. April is Tax Month. It is Reckoning, for render unto Caesar we must.* To keep up with the theme of despots making us ordinary, hardworking folk unhappy with their unreasonable demands, a 2011 ONS survey showed that there have been a disproportionate number of dictators born in April: for example, Adolf Hitler, Saddam Hussein, Genghis Khan and Vladimir Lenin.

On the upside, April, (coming from the verb 'aperire' in Latin, meaning 'to open') is, for the Northern Hemisphere at least, when Nature has downed its double espresso and burst back onto the scene with blossom, bluebells and geese honking and bonking alfresco in the park.

It is the month of Aries (courage, ambition and leadership) and Taurus (determined, lover of beauty, the finer things in life … or materialistic and self-indulgent).

It is the jack-in-the-box month, where everything seems to jump out all at once and you're never quite sure what will come of it. And there lies the opportunity for us all.

---

* Mildly ironic because it was the change from the Julian Calendar in 1752 to the Gregorian Calendar that shifted it to April.

Datus

Wisdom
"April hath put a spirit of youth in everything.".
William Shakespeare

Marketing
Earth Month
National Poetry Month
Usually Easter
1st Fool's Day
23rd St George's Day
10th Siblings Day
13th National Scrabble Day
17th International,
Haiku or senseless poem,
Day of pretension.

Boring Stuff (UK)
5th April Tax Year End UK
6th April Tax Year Start UK (it's
relentless!)

Auspicious time for
Fools!
New starts
Adopting Children (Ch)
Sacrifice (Ch, unclear what ... or who)

Beware!
Ads on TikTok selling financial services

Birthday of Famous Entrepreneur
Bill Gates and Hugh Heffner

Birthday of Inspiring person you've never heard of
Ibn Sina 11th Century Persian philosopher and scientist, often described as the father of medicine. Author of over 400 books, all before laptops and ChatGPT.

Special mention
David Ricardo, Father (or at least favourite uncle) of modern economics

Suscitatio
LEAPING INTO FAITH

Back in April 1992, I felt quite strongly that I was due for a change of luck.

When the chips are down, the trick is to forge ahead trust to fate. I find that generally works for me and it's the main reason I'm sitting here bothering to write an almanack.

First of all, the motorbike, whose state of decrepitude was about to wind me up in court, needed sorting.

There I was helped by Lionel, the ex-husband of the lady who owned the boat I rented, and a thoroughly charming alcoholic. I had always got on well with him and he'd introduced me to lots of other colourfully interesting dipsomaniacs dotted around Chelsea.

When the bailiff came round to the boat to issue the summons, he was greeted by a very affable, possibly tipsy man who told them (on instinct—no prompting from me; I'd never mentioned it) that I had moved away. Boats and pissed people do not make for the impression of fixed living, and the person issuing the papers believed Lionel. And that, dear reader, was the last I heard of that.

But there was the more serious problem of going bust.

Home tuition had hit a ceiling and the margins were terrible (about 10%). Translation, from what I could tell, was a far better option but I had no idea how to go about getting clients.

Providence kicked in again in the form of a chance encounter that changed a great deal.

I was walking about the West End one day and saw a very respectable brass sign on a door. It said something like *MST Translations* or *Worldcomm Translations* and had an engraved globe with what looked like an arrow shooting around it—a bit generic but the brass and mahogany sign itself looked amazing as far as I was concerned. The building was one of those large Georgian affairs you get around Manchester Square, and it gave the impression of dull but secure corporate respectability. I was definitely in clutching at straws mode at that point so, on a whim, I rang the bell and was buzzed up without being asked what my business was.

I climbed the stairs and was greeted by the sight of five guys barely older than me playing office cricket in amongst antique furniture piled with paper and lo-fi computing equipment.

As soon as they worked out I wasn't anyone especially important, I was roped in to playing wicketkeeper. The chap who seemed to be more or less in charge explained between balls that they had started the translation company five years previously on the back of a contract with the EU but were winding up now as the money had gone out of translation and, in any case, they'd already made enough to more or less do what they wanted for the foreseeable future, even if that wasn't very much more than play office cricket.

I decided not to hear the bit about the industry being on the ropes and entirely focus on the idea that I could make piles of money and then get to fritter my time away. I explained that I'd just started out and asked very humbly (for me) if I could mine him for information. If I bought him lunch, he would tell me everything he could he agreed but, he wanted to manage any expectations I had at the outset. 'You'll struggle to make over an 80% margin these days.'

We went to a restaurant in St Christopher's Place and two hours later I felt better than I had in weeks.

As far as I was concerned, 80% margin was pretty bloody good. The important thing was I now had the basic figures in my head, how a project was run, where to find translators and, crucially, where to find clients. I still had a lot to learn but I had the nitty gritties—and I am hugely grateful to a chap to whom I owe so much whose name I've forgotten.

I decided I needed to get a lot more proactive.

I pulled the *Yellow Pages* off the shelf in the office and hit the phones. I'd never cold called in my life, but I had a hunch it was my best option.

I kicked off with people working in hotels.

After speaking to reception in a few hotels and getting nowhere, I made myself a coffee, went to 'M' in the *Yellow Pages* and phoned the first marketing company I saw which was based in Chelsea.

'Hello,' I said, trying to sound cheerful, clever and grave all at once, 'do you ever need interpreters?'

'Not really...' came the response.

'Oh,' I said, already looking at the next company on the page in SW3.

'... but we've just been given the contract to launch the *Jurassic Park* video next year—it's going into thirteen different territories initially and we're looking for a good translation agency. If you're that, your call couldn't have come at a better time.'

Later that morning, I phoned St Mary's Hospital. They were pleased I rang, too, and wanted to see me the following week.

Since then, I have made legions of calls to prospective clients and, back in the old days of fax machines, I would spend my lunch hours with a sandwich in one hand and an A4 flyer in the other, faxing companies in the *Yellow Pages* I thought might want to buy translation services. Like door-to-door selling it's a numbers game and the trick is to work out what those numbers are. Those days, on average, you needed to make one hundred calls (two days' work) to get a client. Therefore, to get two major leads in a morning is vastly fluky.

However, foot in the door or not, I realised my next problem was my age.

With the marketing firm in Chelsea where I pitched for the Jurassic Park work, I was fortunate enough to be pitching to people only two or three years older than me. For the meeting at St Mary's Hospital, the manager in the documentation department came right out and asked, as I walked through the door (jokingly, I hope), if my dad was parking the car.

I made up a title– Business Manager—which gave the impression I was a recently employed salesperson-cum-marketeer with a company that was going places, and not the callow owner of a one-man band with a single rickety desk and phone.

When I went to see the *Jurassic Park* people, instead of asking me questions, then getting a quote and generally taking their time about the process, they told me they wanted to start the following week, and then, as I went out the door, they handed me a strapline *Coming Soon!* to translate into thirteen languages for the next couple of days.

'Does that mean I have the job?' I thought I was just there to chat. In fact, most of the meeting had been about the film and very little had been said about foreign words.

'Yes,' they said, beginning to look doubtful.

'Great!' I said before their doubts found a voice; thinking, *Actually, shit.*

As soon as I got back to the office I wondered where I was going to find someone French, German, Italian, Spanish, Swedish, Estonian, Finnish, Japanese, Latvian, Lithuanian, Romanian, Norwegian and Dutch at very short notice.

I had a think and phoned the Job Centre in Clapham Junction and, surprisingly, that was how I found our first translators and how I carried out our first real translation project.

It was barely a business yet, but the work (and the name, *Jurassic Park*) coming in allowed me to go back to Barclays and get another £2,000, which bought me some breathing space.

May
INSIGNIS

In spite of all the blooming flowers, lofty clouds in robin's egg skies—and the optimism that engenders, May was once considered an unlucky month. Especially if you wanted to get married. It's a bit of a stretch but apparently his had something to do with the Romans celebrating *Lemuria* in May, which their version of Hallowe'en. Luckily, nowadays, we do all that in November, with getting-racier-every-year dressing up costumes (for the mums) and sweets thrown in (for the kids), so we don't have to worry.

Britons, back in the middling-to-olden days, called May *Tri Milchi*, ('Three milking'), which is a rather prosaic way of naming a month in which cows seem to have Space Hoppers for udders.

After all the boring admin of April, May is the month of Truancy: National Holidays left right and centre. And it's International Worker's Day in most countries: celebrating the right of workers to be shirkers. Actually, the eight-hour day labour movement—namely, working for eight hours, sleeping eight hours and dicking around for the remaining eight, is one of the most sensible initiatives around. So long as you don't have to keep stopping to milk your cow.

Datus

Wisdom

"May is the month of expectation, the month of wishes, the month of hope."

Emily Brontë

....

Marketing

Kentucky Derby

National Egg Month

4th May Star Galactic Stars Wars Day

10th World Laughter Day (no doubt hysterical following April tax demand)

12th International Nurses Day

20th May World Bee Day

Boring Stuff (UK)

31st May Last date for issuing P60s to staff in the UK

Auspicious time for

Lollygagging

Weaving a fishing net (Ch)

Taurians

Beware!

Nuptials

Signing Contracts (Ch)

Digging a well (again! Seems you really have to pick your moment in China)

Birthday of Famous Entrepreneur

Mark Zuckerberg

Birthday of Inspiring person you've never heard of

Henry Dunant. Swiss businessman and humanitarian founder of the Red Cross.

Special Mention

Edward de Bono

British Doctor, who solved the problem of solving problems by coming up with the off piste concept of lateral thinking. Thereby being the inventor and first customer of his own theory, so beloved of entrepreneurs the world over.

Conligo
BENNETT'S MUSTER

After five slightly hairy months, the businesses finally got a pulse.

I came across my first cashbook recently, in amongst a pile of life jetsam in the barn of our holiday home, sitting under my first phone—the one I used to annoy people with. The cashbook was damp, slightly warped and I have no idea how it had made its way, down the years and across the English Channel, to France, but it was a record of sorts those early days—pure material fact, no embellishments. Between that and the cheap plastic phone that now looked fetchingly retro I had very little else on or around my one desk 'office'.

It looked like this:

INCOME

January

Nil, nada, zip	

February

£205	London Tutors (commissions)
£400	London Tutors (my home tutoring)
£40	Translation (Yam exporter near the office. First client!)

March

£317.50	London Tutors
£130	London Tutors
£0	Translation

April

£637	London Tutors
£0	London Tutors
£0	Translation

May

£948.75	London Tutors (commissions)
£1850	Translation

Right, I thought—having taken nearly four grand in turnover—now that I'm evidently well on my way to great wealth, it's time to hire someone. Then I'll be just like a proper company.

My first employee was not a success. I can't remember her name, but I wouldn't be surprised if she never actually said. She was a mumbler and, when she wasn't staring at her feet, she gave me hurt looks like I'd just woken her up and dragged her to the office against her will. According to the people who I shared the office with, she stopped work the moment I left the room and only started again, when I came back. I didn't need to sack her because she just didn't turn up after a couple of weeks. About six months later she asked me for a reference.

She was replaced by a girl my age who was doing a PhD and we quickly reverted to student rules of pretending not to take anything particularly seriously and burning the candle at both ends: long lunches, followed by frantic bursts of work late into the night. Things got done, we had a laugh and this felt like just the kind of cavalier venture I wanted to be part of.

Sadly, her PhD wrapped itself up and she got a real job working in Westminster for some sort of quango.

... and then came Margo.

I rented a desk in the far corner of a reception area of forty commercial units at the foot of a sixties tower block. Most of the units were pretty grim, as they made up the basement—like a series of bunkers, enitrely lacking natural light. They housed everything from a recording studio to a tropical fruit importer. My desk, stuck in the corner of the DRCA admin offices, looked out on multiple planes of concrete and tarmac, dotted with sad trees, but at least it had light and free heating. Everyone who worked for the DRCA was female, black and noisy. They routinely ticked me off for: not tucking my shirt in; not complimenting them on their hair; yawning ... made sure I ate lunch at the right time and offered me encouragement.

Into this, Margot turned up as if she'd just stepped out of a Range Rover. A really nice one. Living barely ten minutes walk away, but from another world—one that looked down on Battersea Park from a social vantage of repointed Victorian flats, she monologued for the first five minutes. This included her life, improvements to the way London Tutors worked, random opinions about water features, then cats and an assurance she was prepared to do most things as long as she had free rein to decide how those things were done in the detail.

The unstoppable force of the women who already worked there, measured up the immoveable object that was Margo's personality and quickly decided it was better to unite in disapproval of me.

It was basically like having your mother come and work for you, assuming she smelled strongly of tobacco and swore a lot.

Then my mother really did come and work for me. And then my father ... followed by my big brother.

It happened because the financial hot water they were in had just reached boiling point. The family business had gone bust, which was one thing, but the bank was out for blood and employment opportunities weren't forthcoming at the tail end of a nasty recession.

Strip out the inherent weirdness of becoming the de facto boss of three members of the family who were technically more senior than me, and it kind of made a lot of sense.

My mother was far better than me at talking to other mums about their children's intellectual shortcomings, so she went onto London Tutors bookings. My father is a natural polyglot, plus he had held junior, not-quite-so-junior, middle management and then very senior management marketing and strategic positions for blue chips for thirty years before the current nose-dive. So, he was to spearhead Aktuel Translations' grand entrance into the world of international business and my brother—the least salesy and chatty person in the world—became a kind of anti-salesman. Seriousness equates to sincerity in certain situations. Sales included.

The experience wasn't always easy: it's virtually impossible to carry out an objective appraisal of the sibling you shared a bunk bed with for twelve years and who routinely beat the crap out of you with a plastic lightsabre, or instigate disciplinary procedures on the woman who gave birth to you. Although it did stand me in good diplomatic stead for when my wife started to work for the business after our children came along. All in all, giving me an early and very useful insight into HR, including not losing your shit when your mother mistakenly pays in a whole month's receipts into her own account or your wife prints off all the office banking passwords then leaves them in a health food shop in Wallingford.

Generally, I think too much can be made from the recruitment process.

It's going to put people's backs up, especially those who work in HR, but formal interviews are very often a way to demonstrate that an applicant has read the room, more than their fitness to do the job: a savvy interviewee can give you what you want to hear, rather than need to know. Instead, might I suggest that once you have ascertained that a candidate has the right basic skills or could acquire them in a reasonable amount of time, invite them to hang out in the office for half a day, ostensibly to shadow someone. It's a covert way for you both to decide if it's a fit and dispels any interview nerves that can cloud things.

Like houses, rounds of golf or spouses, you will never find perfection. I'd almost say if you think you have the perfect candidate smiling across the desk at you, then you have probably missed something.

On the upside and with that in mind, if you need to hire but, after a decent-ish interval you can't find the right person, go ahead and hire the next best person who is available (even if they're a blood relation). Fact is, there's a very good chance that person will surprise you (positively). One of the good things about small/smallish companies is the focus you can put into people to get the best from them.

As the Bard said, "Some are born great, some achieve greatness, and some have greatness thrust upon 'em".

And that also includes your first hire—you.

June
INSIGNIS

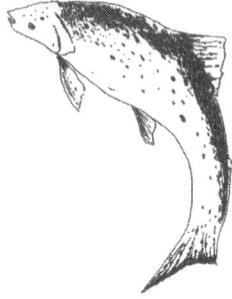

June is historically a month of great leaps into the maw of an uncertain fate: from D-Day, to the signing of the Magna Carta, the inaugural human flight and the first time the world met Donald Duck. What those of us in the Northern Hemisphere know is that this is also virtually the only month in which you can be off to bed and it's still broad daylight.

The ancient Anglo Saxons called it *Sera Monath*, meaning dry month, which proves they had a sense of humour.

For the committed entrepreneur in the UK, more daylight hours mean more people out and about at Royal Ascot, Wimbledon, Trooping the Colour, the start of the Henley Regatta and constellations of fetes, fairs and festivals up and down the country. It's a time to build on budding the sense of growth in May and realise a cornucopia of opportunity.

Fortune fevers the brain.

Datus

Wisdom

"How did it get so late so soon?
It's night before it's afternoon.
December is here before it's June.
My goodness how the time has flewn.
How did it get so late so soon?"

Dr. Seuss

Marketing

National Pollinator's Month
9th Donald Duck Day
18th National Picnic Day
15th Father's Day
19th (busy) Juneteenth, National Watch Day, National Martini Day, World Sauntering Day
21st Summer Solstice Northern Hemisphere

Auspicious time for

Land Wars, apparently
Selling hotdogs and sticky beverages, evidently
Hats, demonstrably

Beware!

Long term barbecue plans in the UK
Poor curtains
Bed installation (Ch)

Birthday of Famous Entrepreneur

Elon Musk

Birthday of Inspiring person you've never heard of

Frank Whittle, English inventor who invented the jet engine in his garden shed. Like many English geniuses, he never made any money from his invention.

Special Mention

Alan Turing, Codebreaker, mathematician and highly-advanced computer scientist

Te Ipsum
THE RULE OF SELF-RULE

It's probably time to tell you about the only proper job I ever had.

Pertinent, because the person I worked for inadvertently taught me two essentials about business. I say inadvertently, because—if asked—he'd probably have liked to have taught me *an enduring love of the classics, nobility of thought* instead ... or *how to iron a shirt*. He was that sort of person. And he seemed to vacillate between having a very low opinion of me and not quite being able to recall why I was even there, to a sort of pensive hopefulness I might, one day, improve.

Peter Boizot was an old-school entrepreneur, the like of which may well be gone for good in this day and age.

Cultured and somewhat hedonistic, he was one of those rare people who can monetise their appetites. In this way food, music and sport translated into him founding PizzaExpress, running the Soho Jazz Festival and owning Peterborough United Football Club. Amongst other things.

None of this I knew at the time I was hired by him, because research was not one of my strong points.

Blithe might be the best way to describe my attitude when I was walking up the stairs of Kettners for an interview a friend had helped me secure. Or—more likely—gloomy. I'd graduated during the 1992 recession and there really were very few proper jobs out there, especially not ones that sounded as interesting as working in the editorial department of a jazz and blues Magazine—another one of Peter's ventures.

Either way, this was one of many, many interviews I'd had in the past year for a job I suspected I had no chance of getting. So I wasn't really hopeful or even concentrating when I wandered through Peter's open door instead of that of the editor at *Jazz Express*.

Two venerable old men looked up from where they were sat enjoying a glass of something. Close by, an expensive-sounding clock ticked, then tocked with authority. After a moment to regroup, they took it in turns to ask who I was, why I was there, and did I also like sherry?

I hadn't had sherry since about 1983, but I took a glass and, discovering I quite liked it became chatty. I explained about the editorial job I was up for, then I talked about the army and the door-to-door selling and somehow Charles Dickens cropped up. The larger of the two men (who also owned the biggest eyebrows), eventually introduced himself as Peter Boizot. Then he picked up a phone and called an internal number. 'Hello Catherine, are you busy? I don't care... Would you come down-stairs for a minute?'

A few moments later, I was being introduced to a girl about my age who was the editor at *Jazz Express*.

'This is Robin,' said Peter, looking like he was getting ready to be magnanimous; 'he'd be a hopeless subeditor and I'm not sure we can afford one—don't you have Gary?'

'Um, yes we do...' Cat started.

'Good, he can just try a bit harder. I think Robin here would be an excellent business manager—not just at PB Publications; he could look into Peroni and the Festival. We'll pay him £1,000 a month. I'm sure he'll be full of ideas.' Peter trained his giant eyebrows on me. 'When can you start?'

'Monday,' I said, feeling pleased and excited, as you do when your life seems to have shifted into a more interesting gear.

I spent exactly a year working for Peter. It was my apprentice-ship in the very satisfying business of turning an idea into cold cash. At the time of my joining, Peter was in deep trouble: the recession had hit PizzaExpress hard, he was mired in debt and it was getting worse every day. However, this didn't stop Peter continuing to do just as he pleased.

Soho was still an interesting place to be, though at its tail end: Jeffrey Bernard was certainly unwell, but he still managed to drag himself to The Coach & Horses next door to our office each day, and could be relied upon to be civil to you if you went in with a pretty girl; Boizot mixed in a wide circle of people so it wasn't in the least unusual to walk into his office and find The Bishop of London sitting there, or the pornographer, Paul Raymond. Just not at the same time.

I got quite good at gatecrashing events at the Groucho and rubbing shoulders with minor celebrities whilst filling my jacket pockets with free sausage rolls.*

Out of this tribe, I quickly found the most entertaining were the writers: Auberon Waugh was grumpy but clever, and would talk to you like an equal—provided you didn't say anything really daft; Julian Barnes was jolly and boyish; Alan Bennett and Stephen Fry competed for being approachable and avuncular. Musicians tended to be a bit twitchy, and actors/TV 'person-alities' would ignore you with a vengeance unless they thought you might be important. One exception being Emma Freud, who breezed into some party at the French House one evening, talked breathlessly at me for about five minutes, like we were old friends, and left—but not before I'd fallen hopelessly in love with her.

Almost the only thing the editorial department of *Jazz Express* and I agreed on was having a dim view of the people we interviewed each month. Peter basically wanted us to fill it full of his jazz friends, most of whom nobody had ever heard of. Instead, we started contacting people like Jamiroquai, Candy Dulfer (Prince's hot saxophonist, and a Grammy award winner in her own right), Jools Holland and David Bowie. The latter, in particular, had never been asked about his jazz credentials in all his born days. We got interviews and lots of free stuff. The front cover we did of Jamiroquai was a brilliant piece of acid jazz design and timed perfectly, just as he was breaking worldwide. He came to lunch and gobbled up half a ton of margheritas with his entourage—but he gave a great photoshoot in that daft hat

---

* It's a regrettable feature of the modern canapé, with its fiddly bits of fennel and lumpfish toppings, etc., that you can't scoop up a handful and put them in your trousers for the journey home. Sausage rolls were ideal scavenging food back in the day for the young man of ambition and no means: compact, transportable and could last for days.

of his. We sold out of that issue and it looked like we were on a roll.

Then Peter stepped in: he strongly objected to the direction the magazine was going, he grumbled. So, we were back to reviewing unknown bands with names like Bobby Bunker and his Jazz Maestros, Davey Dave Davies and The Norfolk Swingers, and trying to sell £25 spot ads to local record shops that usually didn't pay us anyway.

All things considered, it wasn't a bad magazine: some of the writers—especially Larry Adler and Miles Kington—were top-flight, but a lot of it was repetitive month by month or almost impossible to read. After eight months, I decided that, much as I liked free food and knowing some famous people a little bit, trying to make something commercial that didn't want to be was depressing. The upshot was I started to take myself off to the stockroom to read Terry Pratchett books or hide in The Coach & Horses alongside a perennially hungover Jeffrey Bernard, who glared at me over his twenty or so vodka tonics because I didn't have a discernible pair of breasts.

In June, a year to the day after I started at *Jazz Express*, I handed in my notice

I hadn't got a plan for a business as such—but I had something much better: a proven way to go about it when I eventually did.

Because Peter had shown me that good entrepreneurship was not just about having ideas. Primarily, he showed me that there is no rule book. If you hold all the strings (and by that, I mean you own a majority of the business) you can use almost any path that suits you to get to your goal. Smart people (and almost everyone who worked for Peter had been to Cambridge) sat in meetings and gave him elegantly-worded, clever clogs solutions to problems or plans and Peter absolutely always went ahead and did almost the exact opposite. And each time he did these eccentric, tangential things, we'd throw our hands up in horror and exclaim he'd gone potty and it was all going to hell in a handcart. Then, a few weeks later we'd discover he'd been right all along. Not because he was right right, but because he was completely correct in his conviction there are many ways to go about the same thing and the most important thing is to decide what works for you.

And never deviate, since (secondly), after all his trials of debt and people saying he'd lost it, never had it anyway, was too old etc, he'd come out on top, floating PizzaExpress and earning several tens of millions overnight. *He'd taught me to stay the course*.

And it was this insight that was currently standing me in good stead. Even saving my bacon.

July
INSIGNIS

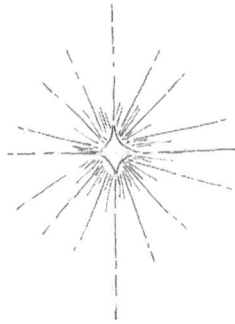

Named after the previously-mentioned Julius Caesar (his surname actually a nickname, meaning 'hairy bloke'). Another hirsute despot was born in July: the famously blond-maned Alexander the Great (hairdo).

These are known as the Dog Days, presided over by Sirius – the Dog Star. Sweltering afternoons scourged by canine rabies that roamed the fly-blown streets in antiquity. July is the month where Crab gives way to Lion (more manes). Bet Samson was a Leo.

With Leo in ascendancy, it is the month for leadership ... and yet more war. The birthstone is the Ruby, which warriors would embed into their armour as protection from blade and bane. Like droplets of blood.

After the call to arms of June, July is the fray.

Datus

Wisdom
"It's July and I have hope in who I am becoming."
Charlotte Eriksson

....

Marketing
National Anti-boredom Month
1st International Joke Day
2nd World UFO Day
7th World Chocolate Day
14th Bastille Day
14th Shark Awareness day (all year,
surely? Ed)
28th World Hepatitis Day!
National Ice cream month

Boring stuff (UK)
6th P11D documents to be issued to
employees and HMRC for tax year UK.
31st Second income tax payment on
account deadline for tax year UK.

Auspicious time for
Seaside holidays and ice-cream
Crushing one's enemies

Beware!
Hairdressers
Buying livestock (Ch)

Birthday of Famous Entrepreneur
The bearded and bouffant Richard
Branson

**Birthday of Inspiring person you've
never heard of**
Rosalind Franklin groundbreaking
work in x-ray technology, viruses and
DNA.

Special mention
Bass Reeves
Inspiration for The Lone Ranger

Fides

BATTLING IT OUT

About a year after I'd quit a pretty decent job in a company that did interesting things with fairly interesting people, things were OK but I was beginning to wonder—with some justification—if thirteen-hour days, six days a week were really worth it.

One evening I remember I had left all my friends in the pub just at that drinking upward trajectory, where everyone had settled into their second pint and were beginning to enjoy themselves about thirty percent more than they had been on their first. I was walking back home to the boat, because I was feeling too broke to drink.

I ought to have been enjoying the walk: it was one of those warm evenings that take you by surprise in London, where the streets, the squares and the parks seem to belong somewhere else, to some southern city in Spain or France. But I wasn't feeling it. I was going back to work and I'd be slogging away on something until just before midnight that probably wouldn't ultimately make much difference to my career or the business. Then I'd go to bed in order to get up at 6.30am to start all over again. I wouldn't have a hangover, that was one consolation after one pint had barely touched the sides, but I wasn't exactly making fun memories out of my glorious youth.

The business existed and I hadn't felt the draw of a convenient ditch to starve in as yet, but I was effectively starting every month with nothing in the bank and having to earn everything I could over the next twenty-two days in order to have enough to pay bills five days later, when the cheques had cleared. It was perpetually nervy.

The problem was my core business—London Tutors—was far too sensible. It was the type that takes time to establish and produced the type of margins designed to keep modest folk in lifelong borderline penury. I hadn't invented something that was going to change the world or even Battersea and I didn't and don't have the bone-headed thick skin, borderline autism to cut it as a disruptor. One bad month I'd be badly winged; two I'd be out of business.

The shadow of slow ruin slunk at the edges of my consciousness, like the type of dog that's just a bit too big and rangy to ignore with equanimity. And it had a companion, even more vague—just a suspicion—that lurked alongside my money worries. I suspected I might be a bit idle.

At the time, as I stomped home in a bad mood, I dressed this sudden negativity up as common sense: almost everyone I knew was earning twice what I did and working half as much. Why was I putting myself through this? All the businesses I knew or read about were either inherited or had piles of seed funding to start with. E.F Schumacher was a dangerous fantasist: small was not beautiful. It was mundane drudgery and probably not worth the candle.

I think there's a moment in everybody's personal story where the dream slips out the door unregarded and reality stomps in, along with a nasty draft.

There's probably two ways of dealing with this when it happens. You can mope about, being a self-pitying prick and start making excuses to throw the towel in, just like I was currently doing … or you can turn around and go back to the pub.

Like I did instead.

Walking home about three hours later I felt much, much better. Not just because I was pissed but I also thought I had a solution to my woes, or at least something that sounded reckless enough to appeal to me as I bounced along on the beer bus looking for a cheap kebab.

I was never going to be able to make a comfortable amount to live off until I could make money whilst I was asleep. Otherwise, I just had a job—where I was the only employee.

The translation side of the business had lovely big margins but getting anything like a regular client base was proving hard. I needed to grow a pair, get rid of all the other stuff that was taking up too much time and trust—yet again—to fate.

But, this time, it wasn't about having faith in my fate, I mused as I stuffed a jalapeno pepper in my mouth. The way forward, I decided, lay elsewhere. I watched my fellow pedestrians through the window of the kebab shop with the benign eyes of a man who has drunk five pints on a largely empty stomach and it dawned on me ... other heavenly bodies! I would overcome my natural urge to do everything my way, let go and trust that other people could be even more productive, successful than me, and catch the odd break occasionally. I'd muster staff—I'd made the breach, now it was time to let them loose.

But, at the same time, I will care for my team like the good shepherd I thought solemnly (whilst now making serious inroads to half a kilo of roasted meat). As we grew, I would make their futures, their hopes and dreams my concern. We would all be happy, empowered and one.

August
INSIGNIS

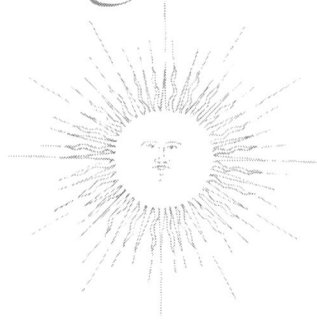

August was traditionally a month of future proofing. Root vegetables and whatnot you planted a few months ago were ready to be crowbarred out of the sun-baked ground and put in jars for winter. Now shoppers have heavily-marketed celebrities paying people to put things in jars for us. So instead, we, in the effete tertiary sector, generally turn off our work emails this time of year and go somewhere just-about-affordable. If you're American you'll do this for one week, British two, French thirty-one straight days with a week either side in which you're expected to be surly and rubbish at your job.

Both preserves and hollibobs are forms of reward, it's just the latter is a lot more fun than the former—unless you find cucumbers hilarious.

Life has improved but August is still the month where the industrious lay the groundwork for winter—the better to appreciate your giant Negroni from a veranda looking out on a sun-hazed beach, endless sea and bottomless sky.

Datus

Wisdom

"August slipped away into a moment in time,
'cause it was never mine."

Taylor Swift

Marketing
International Beer Day (first Friday in August)
International Sandcastle Day (first Saturday in August, provided you're not too hungover)
9th World Orangutang Day
26th National Dog Day

Boring stuff (UK)
Nuffink! Chill.

Auspicious time for
Turnips
Take a bath (Ch)

Beware!
Package holidays
Growing plants (Ch)
Installing a door (Ch)

Birthday of Famous Entrepreneur
Me

Birthday of Inspiring person you've never heard of
Maurice Hilleman developed more vaccines than anyone alive, and kept millions of us alive in the process.

Special mention
John Flamsteed, first Astronomer Royal, first person to map the stars but, most importantly, first person to observe Uranus.

Festum
LIFE'S A BANQUET

I had something to aim at! The London skies' usual low ceiling of grey cloud expanded up and outward; deep blue and boundless. You could say to mirror my rekindled ambition but that would not be true - I was still predominantly concerned with keeping a roof over my head. The grass burnt brown as London emptied of its usual cargo of workers, then filled with *away dayers* in coaches and professional shoppers from oil countries. And I rolled my sleeves up.

Websites wouldn't be a thing for at least a couple of years, so I wrote marketing brochures and what, I hoped, were persuasive letters. I drew up lists of languages we would cover, lists of prices, legal-like terms and conditions, fact sheets, fun facts and free advice for prospective clients about the intricacies of language and the world of translation I hardly knew anything about.

Then I contacted the local Job Centre and a couple of local employment agencies: the former for prospective translators, the latter for the sales team I was going to build. I used the remaining credit I had with the bank to get another £5000 loan, on top of the £3000 I'd already borrowed (and the £30K of student debt).

We were still in the tail end of a recession, so pretty soon I had a reasonable list of linguists and a couple of people my age who I reckoned sounded good on the phone.

With enough money in the bank to keep my crack sales team for around sixty days, starting in September and fix up the crumbling 68' Daimler Sovereign I drove about in those days, the better to go to see prospective clients, I looked about with a degree of excitement and a hint of trepidation.

Then I buggered off on a well-deserved holiday.

Reward is a big part of making risk worthwhile. If your incentive is money, spending lavishly on yourself is proof you don't just have a gambling habit dressed up as a business venture. For others, it is a reasonably prolonged period of sloth (surprisingly expensive). Basically, whatever floats your boat. Hedonism is good and I was quickly realising that none if this was worth doing unless it was somehow fun. Epictetus was right, or if he wasn't he should have been: life is a banquet.

For now, I didn't have any money and therefore neither of the above was an option. I went on a walking holiday in Norfolk instead—on the basis it's closer than Scotland and less hilly.

September
INSIGNIS

For many in the northern hemisphere, September is fast becoming the golden child. A combination of sleepless summer nights, one too many conversations about mosquito bites and school holidays now lasting an eternity (from the fee-paying fraternity) has shanked July and shoved August off his plinth. The sunshine in September feels like a bonus. Finally, you can drift off without stuporising yourself in sweat, or being startled by insects setting off miniature chainsaws next to your ears just as you are on the threshold of sleep.

September is the month of reaping what you sowed when everyone else was stuffing their face in front of a statement barbecue whilst getting sozzled on gin.

It's a time to harvest. With the business ground seeded in August, September forms a vital part of the cycle of business that is never-ending (get used to it). September is sales. People are at their desks and have not quite gotten over the back to school feeling of now. There is never a better time to pick up the phone, turn up to conferences, buy advertising on Google and generally run amok on the back-to-work factor and winds of free trade.

Datus

Wisdom

"September's Baccalaureate
A combination is
Of Crickets — Crows — and Retrospects
And a dissembling Breeze
That hints without assuming —
An Innuendo sear
That makes the Heart put up its Fun
And turn Philosopher."

Emily Dickinson

Marketing
'Second Hand September'!
1st Ginger Cat Appreciation Day (US)
8th International Literacy, Day (UK)
21st International Wife Appreciation Day (Coincides with World Gratitude Day)
22nd International Hobbit Day

Boring stuff (UK)
30th Deadline for filing accounts with Companies House for accounting year ending 31 Dec.

Auspicious time for
Marketing
Cheap mini breaks, if you didn't get away in August

Beware!
Sloth
Adopting Children (Ch)
Tomb (Ch, [unclear what about tombs, exactly])

Birthday of Famous Entrepreneur
Colonel Sanders!

Birthday of Inspiring person you've never heard of
Lewis Latimer
Son of two runaway slaves. Inventor of flushing loo on a train. But, if that isn't enough to stun you (as if!), he also has a claim to inventing the Lightbulb and the Telephone.

Empatia
THE SOLIPSISM OF SALES

For someone in translation, it took me an astonishingly long time before the penny dropped that being local trumps most things, especially when trying to persuade people to buy things from you. I once flew all the way to Shanghai in China trying to do just that. It was in the very early days of China's economic boom in the very late 90's and I'd been talking to Shanghai University about setting up a translation company together. I thought if I was going to branch out, I'd go large. On the way over, I stopped off in bicycle-rammed, car-free Beijing and picked up an interpreter.

The meeting (in a hotel that looked more like the reception of a 19th century printing works somewhere like Liverpool) seemed to go well. In that I said stuff, my interpreter interpreted, and they all nodded and smiled with great enthusiasm. I went home feeling pretty chuffed, thinking it was all going in the right direction.

Then heard nothing from Shanghai University. Ever again.

It took two more trips to China on other business before it was explained to me I should have used a Shanghainese interpreter. 'They probably thought your Beijing interpreter had been sent to spy on them.' I was told by someone from Birmingham who had successfully set up a rubberised playground surface manufacturing partnership out there. 'And they were probably right,' he added darkly.

Sometimes I think sales IS my job (not writing, entrepreneurship, whatever). I've sold contraband at boarding school, sandwiches at university, aerial photographs of people's houses snapped at four thousand feet door-to-door. In Yorkshire of all places. I've sold vodka jelly shots on the street, advertising space in magazines, perfume in Harrods and translation. Lots. Millions and millions of words in scores of languages.

And I've learned that sales is an infinitely more subtle process than is commonly supposed.

The image most of us have is it being the domain of the brash, the over-sharey, the under-qualified. Not that being a bit of a chatterbox is a bad thing in sales, it's just not the only thing. Before I get into how it worked out for us, being liked, or likeable is by far the most important element in sales.

Hardly anyone will buy from you unless they warm to you. If they actively don't like you, they'll think of any reason to avoid giving you money. If they do connect with you in a positive way, they'll generally do their best to maintain that relationship. Sales is human nature accelerated.

It's visceral but it's even more than that—because there's luck involved. To be a good salesperson, you need to do your numbers (calls, visits, pitches etc) and that's fine. To be great, the gods of entrepreneurship must love you.

The hardest working salesperson I ever employed was also the unluckiest.

If Damian were to drop a piece of toast on the floor, not only would it land butter side down every time but, as he bent down to retrieve it, a kitchen drawer would mysteriously slide open, and he'd bang his head on one of its sharp corners when he straightened up.

Damian was going through a rougher patch than usual when I took him on. His girlfriend, he told me on his first day, had left him and he could no longer afford to live where he was. Unable to leave until the lease was up, he was temping wherever he could to make ends meet and spending the rest of his time feeling a bit glum about the fact his life wasn't going as planned—he had a doctorate in something intensely literate. Sincere and amusing in that diffident way English people can pull off, he was very likeable, which is why I kept him on for about a year longer than I should have.

I loved listening to him on the phone. His charm and his ever-so-slight lack of confidence kept prospective clients on the phone longer than the average and he sent out stacks of our brochures. And never closed a single sale in over eighteen months.

We had lots of chats about 'where he might be going wrong', and 'things to improve'. I set him call targets (forty calls a day), which he smashed, had endless discussions about what the letters that went with the brochures should say, attended meetings with prospective clients who seemed keen enough but mysteriously never really crossed the line and bought any translation.

Karly, on the other hand, whilst pretending to be a busy little bee, cut corners all the time. She was smart enough to figure out that, to keep me happy, it was not the minimum number of calls I aimed for a day but the number of meetings she needed to get booked. In under a year, she'd set me up with enough new clients that we were able to afford to move into bigger, proper offices in an attractive courtyard in a quietly respectable part of Battersea.

I thought about it a lot and decided, at the end of the day, Damian wasn't doing anything wrong and Karly wasn't a sales genius. The biggest difference between them was that she firmly believed she deserved to be successful. So she was.

And I saw this repeated time and time again over three decades: successful people are successful because they genuinely can't visualise a world in which they are not. It's a form of solipsism, I guess. The world around you is yours for the conjuring, with you right at the heart of it. Having a ball. It's not necessarily megalomania or ego, as I find these people are often well-balanced and generally considerate of others ... it's just a slightly extreme form of optimism. The gods don't necessarily favour the brave, but they do seem to warm to a sunny disposition.

Sales manuals will often speak about the importance of pitching yourself on the same level as your target market or at least showing you care. In its pure state it's now called 'mirroring'—as practiced by spies and Met Officers infiltrating groups of dangerously-committed vegans. In its crappest arrangement, it's someone selling internet services who phones you up out of the blue and opens with 'How's your Thursday going, nearly the weekend, eh?'/ 'What's up with the weather, mad innit?' etc.

This never, ever fools anyone into thinking the person on the other end of the phone isn't anything but annoying, so I don't know why telesales companies persist.

Truth is, in my experience, the best and possibly only way to be on the same level as your prospective client is to actually be on their level in the first place—or very close.

I once took on a German salesperson. I could never quite figure Silke out: she could have been anywhere between twenty-four and forty, dressed like a well-paid executive in a city bank and ate out in restaurants every lunch time—although I was probably only paying her about £12.50 an hour before tax. She also managed to fit into every lazy stereotype we have of Germans: blond and almost indecently-healthy, abrupt up-to-and-often-beyond-the-point-of-very-rude. And a bit racist to boot (she told anyone who'd listen the rest of Europe should try and be a bit more German and a lot less Greek). This directness extended to ringing clients in Germany up and demanding to know why they weren't already using our translation services and if not, why not.

And they lapped it up. Twenty years later, we still have clients that came from Silke's offensive (in every sense of the word) sales technique.

Back in the UK, in a class-driven society, this means your accent, the words you use, the region you're from, put you in or out of people's bubbles within the first thirty seconds of any conversation. In practical terms, if you're selling Highland cattle to farmers in Scotland, it's probably best not to sound like you come from Guildford. The only thing I found to buck the trend are people from around Newcastle: everyone loves a Geordie accent. Nevertheless, it pays to hire people who most fit your target market.

So that was another one of Damien's 'problems', in that that he wasn't much like 99.9% of the population, unless I had him selling to Oxford Dons and obscure literary critics.

I was genuinely sad when he left but we were now growing so fast, I had other things on my plate. You see, something still didn't feel quite right. On the face of it, the push had worked better than I could have hoped, even at my most optimistic: we had a steady stream of clients coming in, nice offices and nice staff. But I didn't have to dig too deep to see that I still had a lot to learn about running a business. A different sort of trouble was brewing.

October

INSIGNIS

The foundation of the United Nations and Columbus reaching America, the first ever Satellite (Sputnik) and the reunification of Germany all happened in October. It saw the first TV transmission, the first mass-produced, affordable car (Model T Ford). But it also marked the end of the Anglo-Saxons in England (Battle of Hastings), the end of the French Monarchy (Marie Antoinette decapitated), the end of British rule in America. This is the month the first McDonalds opened in the UK.

Poised between summer and winter, might October be a month of beginnings or endings? Perhaps it's better seen for its contradictions and pivots—as a periodical roll of the dice.

At the open, Libras: the most chilled star sign and Scorpios: the most intense, at the close. The birth flowers are marigold for love and cosmos, grief. The birthstones are opal, signifying spiritual purity and tourmaline, material wealth.

Commerce can be a contradiction in itself: things can be simultaneously going well and, in another reading of things, to hell in a hand cart. In a sense, October is a lesson in riding things out towards an uncertain horizon, when one's goal seems blurred and the status quo uncertain.

Datus

Wisdom
"October is a symphony of permanence and change."
Bonaro W. Overstreet

Marketing
ADHD Awareness Mo ... Socktober!
1st Financial Planning Day
2nd National Smarties ® Day
7th National Poetry Day
21st National Apple Day

Auspicious time for
Disruptors

Beware!
Indecision

Birthday of Famous Entrepreneur
Bill Gates

Birthday of Inspiring person you've never heard of
Saint Corbinian: Bear and beer genius. 8th century founder of the oldest brewery in the world in Weihenstephaner. Also famous for making a bear carry his luggage after it had eaten his mule.

Special Mention
Kongō Shikō, founder of the world's oldest documented company, Kongo Gumi in 578CE, making it over 1400 years old. Have built and maintained Japan's most iconic temples, shrines, and castles, including Osaka Castle.

Attende quid vultis
KNOWING THYSELF

It's 7am and I'm hiding behind a tree outside our block of flats in Clapham, whilst trying to look like I'm not really hiding at all. Almost all the late summer warmth has drained out of the sun, so I'm freezing my nuts off. This is not helped by the fact all I've got on is a wet towel and an even wetter pair of swimming trunks.

I'm twenty-four but I'm waiting for my mum with the same level of anticipation I reserved for end of terms when I was eight at boarding school.

She's got a spare set of keys, which I'm desperate for as I've locked myself out of my flat when I went down to the basement of our flat for my morning swim and sauna. The porter very kindly let me use his phone to ring her, but his altruism didn't extend to letting a half-naked man drip in his office.

So here I am.

Ironically, this point in my life was probably the closest I got to being on a trajectory towards real wealth and distinguished success. The slightly undignified image of me skulking in the bushes could be superimposed with another from the week before, where I am sitting in the back of a chauffeur-driven 1950 Phantom IV Rolls on my way to supper at Bibendum in Chelsea.

Conquest and calamity had become the twin states of my existence: winning clients we were really good at, keeping them happy was proving a challenge, remembering anything else in my life impossible.

Problems at work were sometimes down to straight quality control where we were fast learning that translators had to be checked, then checked again. The week before The Tate Gallery in London had unfurled an impressive banner, some eight foot by ten printed on Sea Island cotton or something equally dear.

60

It was tethered from the top of the Millbank domed entrance to its marble floor and bore the message 'Welcome' in dozens of languages. Except it didn't. 'Bienvenue' had been spelled wrong, a fact that was almost immediately pointed out by some linguistically outraged French tourists.

Sometimes bad things were happening because I was naïve in a pre-internet industry that still relied on a pool of relatively local talent who could be capricious. I'd been racing along the M4 to a meeting one day and had received a phone call from a Mandarin translator who had told me he'd woken up that morning and decided to double his prices ... and (he added, sounding like he didn't give a fuck what I was going to say next), he'd also decided to ask for money up front on a job that was already late.

And sometimes we were just plain unlucky. A Norwegian job we were doing for a big tractor making client had gone off the rails when the translator had done exactly that and ended up in hospital after a train crash with a broken jaw and several other more minor but probably quite painful injuries.

Either way, I was firefighting almost all the time and feeling permanently hare-brained about everything else, which meant that finding myself standing half-naked in the street first thing on a Tuesday morning seemed about par for the course in those days.

It wasn't helping that I seemed to think it was important to keep coming up with new business ideas. That autumn, I'd decided that with a relatively healthy bank balance the best thing was to start a school for boys in Central London. Because I knew nothing about schools and how they were founded/run and I had almost no time to plan it, I put an offer in on the first property I looked at. It was the old Post Office workers' Union building in Lambeth and there was a big private residence next door that came as part of the deal I could rattle around in until someone decided to marry me and have thirteen children.

In hindsight, it was not a bad idea and the property was perfect, with its parquet floors, assembly area and many Edwardian offices. There was a paucity of good boys' schools in London and a plethora of parents, in those days, with plenty of cash to afford the fees that would make it viable.

Luckily (or unluckily) Lambeth Council refused planning on the basis I wouldn't be employing enough people (I think they also hated the idea of something so previously socialist being used to foment toffs right under their noses).

I was disappointed but I'd also made my first serious foray into publishing and had put a call out for 'new and interesting authors' who hadn't been published. So, when I wasn't trying to learn how to run a start-up translation company that had suddenly become rather international, I was reading scores of manuscripts by authors writing everything from fantasy to gay BDSM fiction.

And perhaps I was over-doing the hedonism, too. I was coming to learn that just because I had the money, didn't mean I needed to spend it immediately on the first thing that sounded like fun. I needed a thoughtful hobby, like beekeeping or something that involved honing wood.

I think it was Aesop who said *Be careful what you wish for in case it ends up happening and you're too young and stupid to rein it all in.* Or words to that effect.

November
INSIGNIS

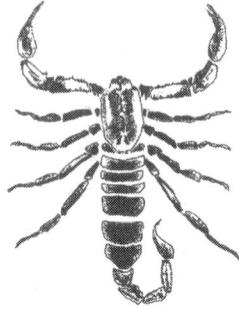

November feels like the dark side. The House of Scorpio is ascendant: severe, demanding and, perceivably, narrow in mind. It is the mean-spirited month ... if we let it. The darkening days are accelerating towards a bit of a low point or tipping into an abyss—depending on the level of your SAD. Everything in nature is either muddy or frozen or something somehow worse that's in between.

But there is hope and that comes in the form of attack. Offensive manoeuvres against a season that can seem crude and cold are the best foot forward. Get out and about and get over it—the damp and the dark are dispelled by Victorian values: vigorous activity where hands can be seen at all times and a decent log fire at the end of it.

For this is the month for bonfires, one way or another. Put to torch the deadwood and bask in its warmth and light, in its last gift. And when what is no longer vital turns to ash, it nourishes the new.

Datus

Wisdom
"I have come to regard November as the older, harder man's October."

Henry Rollins

Marketing
3rd National Sandwich Day
5th Fireworks Day!
11th Remembrance Day
19th World Toilet Day
30th St Andrew's Day

Auspicious time for
Buying single-use plastic dressing up costumes off Amazon
Sacrifices (Ch)
A haircut apparently (Ch)

Beware!
Cheap dressing up costumes near open flames
Building a ship (Ch)

Birthday of Famous Entrepreneur
"Adi" Dassler who founded the German sportswear company Adidas (younger brother of Rudolf Dassler, who founded Puma—Christmasses must have been interesting).

Birthday of Inspiring person you've never heard of
George Boole (1815-1864), uneducated (in the formal sense) son of a Lincolnshire cobbler. Linguist, mathematician and poet, the algebra he developed remains essential to the design of circuits and computers today. Considered one of the founding fathers of AI.

Special Mention
Mansa Musa, West African king, ruler of the Mali Empire in the 14th century who is thought to be the richest person to have existed. It is estimated he had more wealth than the Forbes' five richest billionaires combined of today. Main source of wealth—gold.

Aequilibrium
FINDING YOUR LEVEL

So, eventually, I got out of London. Not that the place was a problem—far from it—but leaving turned out to be a solution.

Having too many clients (of the wrong sort, admittedly) and not really knowing how to manage them properly is a surprisingly difficult problem to solve. Partly because when all your efforts have been trained on acquisition, it's bedwettingly counterintuitive to just go the other way and start telling people who give you money that you don't like them anymore. Also, common sense dictates that pulling off the same growth trick again but with less less-demanding clients is not going to happen. You don't get lucky twice.

However, the problem with superstition is it's almost always entirely negative and that's a terrible thing in business. People even say a bit of circumspection is a good thing but that's almost always not true. A bit of circumspection above the surface, for all the world to see, usually belies a whopping iceberg of self-loathing, fear and doubt below the surface. And that's a very bad thing indeed.

It's much better to be entirely positive—stupidly so. As long as you're almost pathologically single-minded and you work your arse off, you'll come up trumps.

I'd started out living on a modest boat amongst lots of posh houses in Chelsea to living in a modest cottage amongst lots of posh boats in Henley-on-Thames (via a flat in Battersea). Then I took the decision to move the office to Henley in the run up to Christmas—so we could be properly parochial.

After that, I set about culling those bad clients—the ones who paid us late or rang us up at teatime on Friday with unreason-able demands or asked us for money off because someone in accounts who often went on holiday to Germany thought one of our translations read 'a bit like they had been done by a machine'. Unsurprisingly, these were often the same client.

Then I bought a dog.

What followed was an unnerving state of affairs where I was back to wondering if we had enough money in our bank account most Mondays and I might have persuaded myself more than once (a day) I'd made a terrible decision. I do remember a lot of early mornings, where I woke with a start ... and fretted until it was time to get up. Like a lot of people, most probably.

However, a couple of things happened to make it bearable. Firstly, one of my biggest fears that I'd have to terminate people's contracts because I couldn't pay them anymore since I'd set fire to the company sort of went away when half of them left. We'd always employed people straight out of Uni and I've come to realise most people treat their first job on graduation as a stepping stone to give themselves time to look about, decide what they want to do where and, to a surprisingly large degree, with whom. There's so much transition in their lives, they normally totter off after a couple of years. And that's fine. Especially then.

Secondly, my new, living-in-the-country modus operandi, which included Friday afternoons off, was very relaxing, which helped me relax. The dog helped.

By degrees the translation, tuition, publishing and other bits n' bobs took on a newer, nicer character. As I've said before—or something like it—same as any creation, businesses have soul. This one reflected its new riparian environment: it kept its course (profitability—*just!*) but proceeded calmly, like the Thames and its tributaries do in this part of the world. I loved that change: the refutation of the frenetic, and I've done my best to maintain that sense ever since.

December
INSIGNIS

Ah, that's more like it! If we didn't have a yonder star, a cosy setting ... a baby and an excuse to be cheerful and nice to people, we'd have to make the whole thing up.

Either way, from the first time we as humans started to look at what the sun was up to, December has been a time of hope (that the sun would come back) and gratitude, from about 22nd, when it did. Both these eminently-likeable states of mind have the fringe benefit of being contagious—in a good way—so everyone gets the benefit of the general bonhomie wafting about. And that's good for us, good for the ones we love/like a bit and good for business.

Datus

Marketing
2nd Small Business Day
5th International Ninja Day
10th Nobel Prize Day
11th International Mountain Day
15th International Tea Day

Boring stuff (UK)
30th Self-assessment deadline for
self-employed UK

Auspicious time for
Avarice and gluttony dressed up as
good will. But dressed up very well.

Beware!
Uncles

Birthday of Famous Entrepreneur
Walt Disney

**Birthday of Inspiring person you've
never heard of**
Ada Lovelace author of the first
computer code (to go with the first
computer developed by Charles
Babbage).

Special Mention
Charles Babbage, London-based
mathematician. Responsible for
designing and building a 'difference
engine', and later an 'analytical
engine', both of which were
forerunners to the modern digital
computer.
Also Isaac Newton, arguably the
greatest scientist the world has ever
known.

Bene Facis

HONOURING THE GODS WITH GIFTS

An awful lot of things happened in that first frantic period. By dint of replay through the somewhat grubby optic we call hindsight, when the dust had settled, I realised I had much to be relieved about, if not very grateful.

If I were to make a spreadsheet of those early days with two columns: one for the things I did right and one for all the mistakes, without a doubt, the 'B' column (for 'Balls!') would require some scrolling. And when you got to the bottom of it, you'd be left wondering *how the fuck?* I know I am.

I've never enjoyed hearing that expression 'You make your own luck', especially about myself because, as said, I know loads of people who work really hard, always do the right thing and never seem to get a break. The only wild card that seems to count when life looks very bad indeed (as it will) is held by those happy people who have the constant conviction that their luck will change. And I'm aware that this is another way of saying I'm probably quite shallow: vacuous optimism works for labradors and characters in Disney movies, but it should have no place in the world of business. Yet, it seems, that it does and that there is courage in convictions.

Three years ago, I felt I'd done everything I could in the world of translation and turned the last company I'd started and still owned into a trust to be owned and managed by the staff. Apart from one or two sleeping partnerships, this more or less meant an early-ish retirement at fifty-four, almost exactly thirty years after I started The Bennett Group of companies.

As it happens, it took me just six months to realise that getting up late, walking the dog, then going out for dinner is great but...

So, I cast about for the least stressful company I could start and came up with gardening.

Not real gardening, my new purpose in life is to make things shorter (grass, hedges, the day...). There's very little stress involved, there's an immediate return on what I do—in that lawns, hedges and bushes generally look a lot better for me having made an appearance. And there's prompt payment for hours worked, which is a novelty. Added to all this, I get to drive around in an old Land Rover with the dog next to me. It's perfect for now.

Aside from that, I try and live life the way I've always lived it (other tomes in this series, namely *Fieldsports, Foraging and Terrible Ordeals*, or *The Good Snooze Guide of Great Britain* are a pretty good indication as to what that might be). And writing has been a constant since before all the swashbuckling entrepreneur stuff.

It's been a long haul, but I'm very lucky and, I hope, sufficiently thankful for my lot in life. But gratitude is best shown, not told.

Deosque donis colimus, we honour the gods with gifts—and the only one that counts in their book is belief in their divine providence.

As for horoscopes, astro-profiles—including our *Old Moore's Almanack* at the start, (which is now two and a half centuries in continuous publication)—these might derided as being here for the hopeful, as cosmic crutches for credulous but they endure because they are fun if you don't take them (or yourself) too seriously. And, yet, there is also real power in them. Because belief in celestial order and in the ordained, brings with it pluck and audacity ... without which, being an entrepreneur is well-nigh impossible—and a lot duller.

When you run a business, work hard, look at things with a clear eye but allow for the fact that will only get you so far: faith in the unfathomable, in yourself and, perhaps most importantly, in others, gets you over the line.

Believe me.

When Robin grew up, he thought he wanted to be a soldier until everyone else realised that putting him in charge of a tank was a very bad idea. He then became an assistant gravedigger, a private tutor to the rich and famous, entrepreneur ... until finally settling down to write improbable stories to stop his children killing each other on long car journeys. He once heard himself described on the radio travel news as 'some twit' when his car broke down and blocked the rush hour traffic around Marble Arch. This is about right. Robin is married with three children, one of whom illustrated this book. He spends his time between France and England.

Jude spent most of his formative years in the south of France where it was uncertain that years of inattentive doodling in lessons would come to any use. However, when he was asked to illustrate his second book, a degree in modern languages was beginning to seem a less profitable enterprise by comparison. When not on a muddy building site, Jude enjoys many ordinary things like playing the guitar, rugby and walking his dog along the river. Although he grew up in France, he now spends his days in Bristol where he studies and where the earnings of this book will be spent in its finest drinking establishments.

For more books by
Robin Bennett

visit

www.robinbennett.net

or catch up with him on social media

@writer_robin

For talks or enquiries email

press@monsterbooks.co.uk

MONSTER BOOKS

also by

Robin Bennett:

Fieldsports, Foraging and Terrible Ordeals

Illustrations *by* Jude Bennett

MONSTER BOOKS

January

IN WHICH A GOOSE IS COOKED

When I was about seven years old, my father woke one morning and told us, in all seriousness, that not another day could go by without him tasting the sweet flesh of a goose.

He packed me, our cairn terrier, Judy, and his shotgun into our rusting Morris Marina and strapped a canoe onto the roof rack. Then he set off for the river.

I had my doubts even at the early stages of this enterprise: it was January and freezing cold. On top of this, my father had never expressed a craving for goose before, so I felt pretty sure it would soon pass if the call was left unanswered. However, at seven years old, you just kind of go along with things—especially if your father is anything like mine.

We arrived at a bleak stretch of the Thames somewhere near Reading and prepared everything whilst watching the flock of Canada geese lounging about on an island in the middle of the river. Then we got in the canoe: me at the front with the dog; my father at the back, armed to the teeth.

The few walkers who were braving the weather that morning jumped in the air and looked about in alarm as the first shot rang out. Only the goose my father had picked for his dinner seemed unperturbed, as the pellets simply bounced off the thick mattress of breast feathers from twenty yards away.

Undeterred and completely unaware of the sharp looks he was getting from the bank, my father reloaded and paddled closer.

When the second shot rang out, taking the unfortunate goose's head off, people really stopped to stare.

Several things happened rather quickly after that:

My father (still armed) jumped out of the canoe, retrieved a limply flapping goose and threw it on my lap; he then jumped back in, sliding the shotgun down the side of the canoe; whereupon the shotgun's second barrel went off, with a sort of muffled bang; *and we started to sink*. My father panicked: he threw me onto the bank of the island, along with the dog; paddled as fast as he could across the river in a leaking boat; jumped out of the canoe with the shotgun in one hand, the dead goose in the other; and scampered towards the car.

Then he drove off.

It had been an eventful few minutes, but the next part of the morning went very slowly indeed as I stood on that cold island with the dog and wondered what would happen next.

Eventually a put-upon-looking lockkeeper appeared on the opposite bank, got into a small motor launch and made his way across to where I stood. He picked me up, muttering something about a phone call, and took me back to shore to meet my father – who'd had time to go home, wash the blood off and hide the goose.

Two weeks later, we would be sitting in front of the TV with trays on our laps watching Tom Baker being Doctor Who and stuffing our faces with goose. The whole operation was pronounced a great success.

also by

Robin Bennett:

The Good Snooze Guide of Great Britain

Illustrations *by* Jude Bennett

MONSTER BOOKS

November

Place
Hadrian's Wall.

Yes, but where, exactly?
Sycamore Gap, before it was massacred.

Time of day
The horizon smudged blue grey as dusk settled in on the landscape.

Conditions
Dry but you need layers and a warm dog. Or any other friendly mammal.

Drifting off pleasantly
Easy peasy.

Assisted by
Nothing but fresh air and a sense of boundless freedom.

Dreams?
Vivid scenes of recent events replayed. Awoke with a minor convulsion.

Revelations?
I always thought this wall was more symbolic. It's not. And perhaps I should start bringing one of those airline pillows on these outings.

Upon waking
Scoffed an Aero.

Overall rating
Pointy but refreshing.

FIELDNOTES

Hadrian's Wall is an elusive stone serpent. It slides behind Northumbrian hills and into Northumbrian hollows, hugging the landscape before disappearing from sight into dark, Northumbrian woodland. I have crossed its path dozens of times and only briefly spied this pagan snake of stone that separated the modern world of Pax Romana from The Chaos: the sheep stealers and hairy, angry men. The scorners of togas and totalitarianism.

Usually, by this stage of any car journey between the Home Counties and a brief holiday in Scotland, the idea of stopping the car to look at something you're not quite sure is where you expect it to be lacks appeal. This is especially so when measured against the strong possibility of a blazing fire in the hotel bar on the shores of Loch Lomond.

But today would be the day I finally got to grips with it.

I got up early, chucked the dog in the back of the car and set off; hoping the embers of the Indian summer we were having wouldn't splutter out as we ventured north.

My goal (the one right after I'd accidentally-on-purpose stopped for a MacDonald's breakfast) was the town of Brampton: achieved if you put your foot down and head straight at Carlisle, then ricochet off its suburbs, sort of North by Northeast. The A69 is one of those long roads that could almost be in the USA (if the USA had farms with Viking-sounding names and the Pennines for a backdrop). It's also got the cheapest petrol station ever – somewhere between Brampton and the Roman Fort of *Vercovicium*.

This sounds like a failed brand of cough medicine but is, in point of truth, the largest surviving Roman Fort on the wall that generally had them at intervals of seven and a third miles with mini ones in between to make sure nobody common snuck across it. This wouldn't have been easy, given it was fifteen foot high in most places.

The Roman Command structure must have loved walls and the whole business of populating them with soldiers from the far-flung reaches of their empire. But, when they weren't keeping busy, they were also big on sleep, rightly feeling that you couldn't successfully carpe your busy deum of massacring the locals then dishing out law, order and conjugating, unless you'd had a good six hours rest at night and a midday snooze.[2] In fact, they're likely to have invented the siesta, the Spanish word being derived from the Latin word *hora sexta* "sixth hour" (counting from dawn, whence they retired to their couch at midday).

Or, at least, they claimed they invented it – same as they did with columns, sandals and free speech.

I parked the car in an empty carpark at the Vercovicium site (aka Housesteads Roman Fort), then had a short moral tussle with myself over whether to pay for parking out of season. To take my mind off all that guilt, I reflected that sleep must have been a boon for the legionnaires – plucked from blazing hot Mediterranean and North Africa states and plonked all the way up here to fight angry, cold people.

Unlike them, I couldn't very well warm up by asserting my superiority violently on the passing German hikers encased head to toe in man-made fibre or the elderly couple who smiled at me and said hello as they tottered past, so we set off up the hill instead, passing the Roman ruins at the virtual jog of those that have been in the car too long.

That did the trick.

Cooper (scruffy spaniel) who had the wind up his tail, forked left and dived into a thicket. There was a flurry of activity followed by the exit of an improbable pheasant that complained loudly as it flew low up the rest of the hill then loped over what was my first proper sighting of The Wall. I was warm enough by now to stop and lean against the cold stone cobbles that make up its flanks, recalibrating to the level of emptiness around these parts that never fails to take me by surprise as I assume England is going to have some sort of building everywhere you look.

Yet, seemingly endless humps of small hills abound – green then greying into the distance – ferned valleys, strewn with rocks the colour of old bone and small woodlands deployed like regimental defensive squares. And very much part of it all, by virtue of building skills and their sense of practical aesthetics, the roman wall, far from home but very much at home.

For the next sixty minutes, I walked alongside it, on it, slightly removed from it and eventually came to my destination, the familiar dip and tree where Kevin Costner made friends with Morgan Freeman back in 1991, hardly central to the Robin Hood story but that scene somehow entering into cinema history by virtue of place.

Apart from a few cows, like fluffy teddy bears, and a couple who asked to me to take their picture, there was no-one else in sight, so I got out my picnic of processed meats, crisps and popular chocolate bars, and munched away very happily, chucking bits of pork pie and cheap salami at the dog in between mouthfuls.

By and by, I finished up and made myself comfortable against the ancient wall itself and fell asleep almost immediately.

It was an intrinsically healthy siesta.

Cooper woke me with a succession of sneezes – his way of telling me he is keen to get going. But it was just as well, as dusk beckoned, I was getting cold and rocks that definitely weren't there when I fell asleep had grown out of the ground and were sticking into my kidneys. I guessed I had about thirty minutes of real light left, plus a few minutes of fringy-vestigy stuff I could count on given the expanse of sky and lack of cloud.

In the end, I had fifteen minutes of glorious sunset, then darkness and stars as I arrived back at Homestead Fort and turned downhill towards the silent visitor centre and my lonely car.

I was off to Durham next stop, where my hotel was ... and beer.

Printed in Great Britain
by Amazon

acbb103e-1ef6-46ff-9897-3d4ab4137890R01